ROAD MAP

Poems, Paintings, & Stuff

Kēvin Callahan

Flying Ketchup Press
Kansas City, MO

*I'm a travelin' man, I've made a lot of stops all over the world.
Yes, I'm a travelin' man, whoa I'm a travelin' man...*

Ricky Nelson, 1961

South Africa · Zimbabwe · Amsterdam · Alaska · Germany · England · Spain · France · Itay · Hawaii · Mexico · Canada · Ireland · Switzerland

N
W E
S

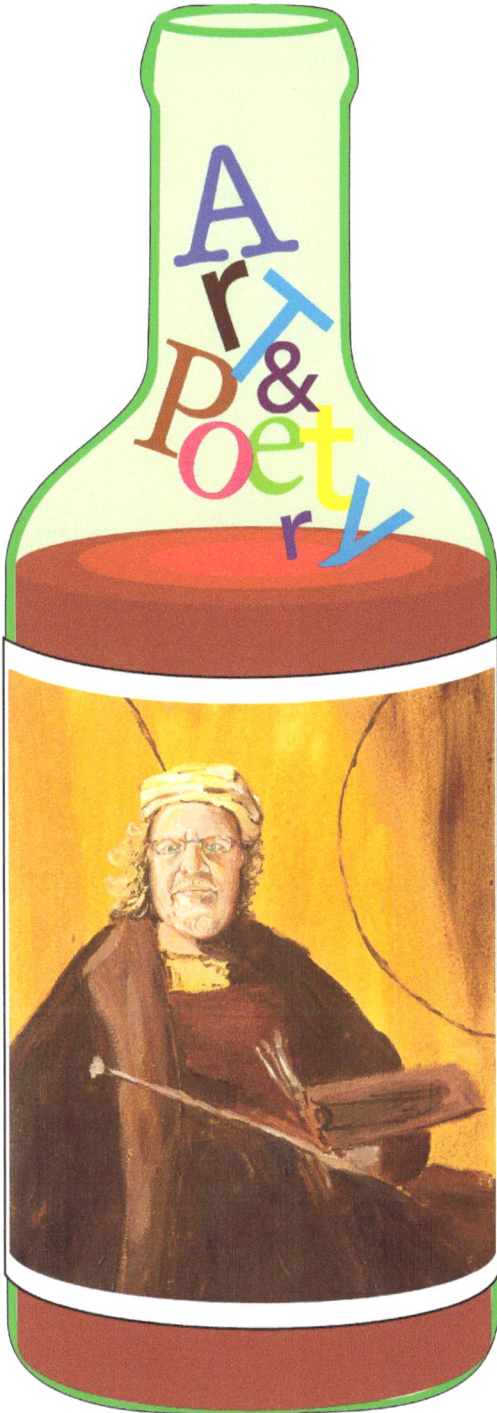

Art & Poetry

WILDLIFE

Portrait of
the Artist as
Rembrandt,
2010

Birds Laughter in the Snow

A singular honk, honk interrupts
the silence and my labors

I pause to reflect, leaning
heavily on my shovel

Gazing upwards, I see
a Vee of wild geese
knifing through a sky
the color of unpolished silverware

January of the New Year has
delivered unto us a wave of weather
ten degrees, I am on day two of
moving snow to create room for more

Looking across the hills the
white, white blanket is punctuated
by winter-dead trees
haphazard exclamation points

I resume my Sisyphean task
the aluminum of the shovel
sounds a *scritch, scritch*
against the concrete walk

Exposing the final bit of stone
a murder of crows caw
their mocking laughter
as it begins again to snow

Doing Battle with Old Bones

During a drive by fruiting last night
two ghoulish denizens died a gruesome death
leaving only oozing intestines of broken jack-o-lanterns

The act undoubtedly perpetrated by
a gang of delinquent deer
showing absolutely no fear of the occult
or my dog

Jack frost was on the prowl
our lawn blanketed with discarded flora,
foliage thoughtlessly dropped to blow and roll
make sounds like old finger bones rattling in the bushes

Donning my armor,
I seize lance and sword
mount my green Deere
and sally forth to do battle

I herd the leaves into long windrows
galloping my green horse
in tighter and tighter ovals and didos

Rake, load, dump, repeat

Rake, load, dump, repeat

Rake, load, dump, repeat

Passing from the forest to civilization
I am greeted by the gift of color

The cotton white of my dog contrasts
with the emerald green of the not yet dormant lawn
glowing like a great jewel in the soft fall light

Carpe Diem
The battle is fought

Winter will arrive in his inexorable creep
but for today warmth and color
have seized the day

Wild Winter Passing

Wily wild turkeys in single file descend
the rocky defile into the snowy woods
mincing their way like a group of old ladies off to tea

Mighty hawk perches on a carcass surrounded
by a Swiss guard of bronze-backed gobblers
clucking softly, scratching white turf for yellow kernels

Young buck bounds breakneck across a winter field
challenges fate as he hurdles between cars
unscathed, he kicks his heels in triumph

A coven of crows in a circle, croak prayers
to the bald eagle, their God/King, ruler of the kill
feeding on the bits and pieces of a long winter

We pass on into the white mist
recording the memories of
these scenes of wild winter passing

The Ant's Picnic,
Spoon Sculpture,
2017

In the Desert Gloaming

In the desert gloaming
silver sage shivers over
purple wildflowers

Cholla cacti lives and dies simultaneously
dead skeleton arms embracing
living branches bearing golden tiaras

Rocks large and small lay mute
not so the desert floor
singing its song in mini riots of color

This desert is a symphony of life
where once a year
even the thorns wear crowns

In the desert gloaming
silver sage shivers over
purple wildflowers

Phenomenon

You hear them before you see them
a sound in the breeze like
the striking of one thousand ivory chopsticks

A black Tsunami rolls in blocking the sun
grackles drop to the ground like ebony leaves

Flakes of pepper season the lawn in search of sustenance
Startled, they soar in unison to some unknowable command
then settle back to the soil

In the midst of the sudden midnight, a single bird
with snow-white tail feathers feeds and flies with his fellows
A phenomenon, does he know he is singular?

As quickly as it arrived the black storm blows away
with the sound of one thousand ivory chopsticks

monkey, Monkey, MONKEY!

Victoria Falls, Zimbabwe, Africa

In the year 2000, my wife and I had the trip of a lifetime. We were in South Africa for the International AIDS conference. Her company sent her as part of her job. I got to tag along. Since we were spending two weeks in South Africa, we thought we might take an extra week and go on a photo safari. Zimbabwe was the most likely place, and the company helped set up some of the details. There were 32 of us scheduled for the safari. Unfortunately, our safari coincided with the political unrest in Zimbabwe. By the time we got to Johannesburg, SA there were two of us, Karen and me.

Our first stop in Zimbabwe is Victoria Falls for a couple of days before we go on a photo safari in Hwange national park. The Victoria Lodge is a beautiful hotel designed to mimic a hunting lodge. Set into the side of a hill, the hotel is arranged so that all of the rooms face a forested waterhole. Guests observe and photograph all types of wildlife when they come for water. The grounds are crawling with monkeys, and we are cautioned not to leave our balcony doors open, as the monkeys will come inside and rifle through luggage. It is also understood that they will bite. I don't remember what type of monkey but they are certainly cute. Adults are about the size of a five-year-old child, gray/black, lean, and in possession of long sharp fangs.

We spend two lovely days boating on the Zambezi River, looking at the falls, riding wild elephants, and in the most surprising of all, dinner with two friends from New York who have checked into our hotel. It is a small world.

In the mornings, I sit on the balcony drinking coffee and smoking my pipe. I take time to write and sketch. Often just watching the parade of wildlife coming to the waterhole. Several monkeys come within a couple of feet of the balcony and look at me as I look at them.

It is early in the morning on the day we are leaving for Huange to join our photo safari. My turn in the bathroom, and I am buck naked with half a face of shaving cream when I hear Karen frantically screaming.

"Kēēēviiin! monkey, Monkey, MONKEY!"

What the hell? I step out of the bathroom to see what-is-what when Karen shoots by me like she has a monkey on her butt. She leaps into the bathroom, closes and locks the door! In our small room, by the bed, is one adult male monkey. He begins to open one suitcase, and another monkey is on the way through the open door. I closed the doors but did not set the inside latch. These little buggers are clever.

For one long moment, three naked apes take stock of each other. I have no idea what they think of a pink, hairless, fat, middle-aged human with foam on half his face but I am certainly intent on those long sharp fangs.

"Hey!" I yell sharply. "You get out of here!"

The monkey by the door shoots out onto the balcony and back into the trees. Monkey number one does not move. He takes a very long look at me, then gives me what seems to be a shrug of the shoulders and saunters out the door, a picture of complete insouciance.

It takes me longer to get Kare to unlock the bathroom door than it took to vanquish the wild beasts from our room. On that, we had a good laugh. But there are greate adventures yet to come.

Pencil drawings
from the
Sketchbook,
2000

7

The Visitor

I had a visitor while watering the plants today
an emerald dart, a hummingbird
no bigger than a moment
quicker than a thought

The avian jewel appeared from thin air
inches from my startled countenance
in what was either a greeting or abject curiosity
a long moment - then gone (into space and time?)

I resume my Aquarian task my gem rematerializes
returning to the courtyard again and again
I gaze rapt as he pierces the delicate blooms
drinking sweet nectar from each, one by one

What a gift for us both
Mother Nature's elixir for him
a moment of avian magic for me

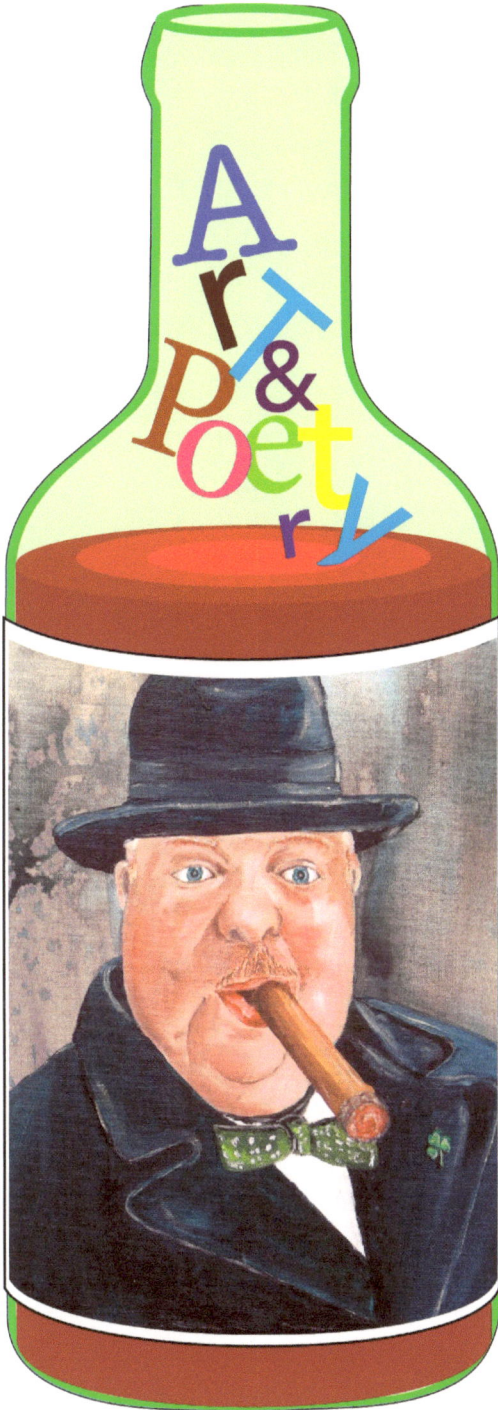

Portrait of
the Artist
as Winston
Churchill,
2014

INTROSPECTION

FatMan Ponders

Old FatMan sittin' on his deck
both his dogs givin' him heck

First he pets one then pets the other
finally gives up and pets em both together

Give em each a bone and lights a big cigar
rockin' an thinkin' in his lawn chair

Smiles as the train horn blows down in the hollow
clickety clack on the track where the engine goes
     the cars must follow

First warm day makes him think it's pretty nice
not to be lookin' on a world of snow and ice

Reflections While at Work

I went into the yard
to rake the mown grass
and dead summer leaves

Is there anything sadder than
those fallen before their time
amid the green of their brethren?

After a few vigorous strokes,
my shoulder begins to ache
my body betrayed by its age

I begin to stroke the grass slowly, softly
like brushing the hair of your lover

Soon, I am done,
my task complete

Leaf,
Graphite
drawing, 2010

Sitting on the Edge of the World

Sitting on the edge of the world
I watch a massive storm move
across an angry ocean leaving hail and
pigeon-egg-sized raindrops in its wake

Sitting on the edge of the world
I watch the roiling sea throw itself
against the rocks with enough force
to spray the grass at the top of the cliff

Sitting on the edge of the world
I see the gentle doe and the
strutting wild turkey. I hear the honk
then spy the mating pair of geese
glide to the ocean's edge

Sitting on the edge of the world
I see the rain then sun and rain yet again
finally, a magnificent rainbow when
at last the warming orb wins the battle

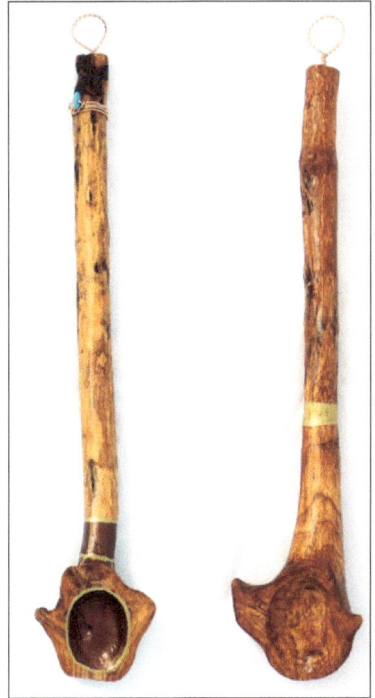

Knot But A Twin,
Two spoons
sculptures from a
single tree knot, 2017

Sitting on the edge of the world
the setting sun glides from under a cloud
splitting it into two perfectly matched planets
until the sky turns crimson and the pale
blue of the virginal bride's dressing gown

Sitting on the edge of the world
I set down my cigar take a sip of bourbon
and watch a jet wing across the horizon
moving from one civilization to another

I know this has nothing to do with me—
sitting in a chair in Mendocino
on the edge of the world

There is a Distance

There is a distance
not far across

So close in fact
a brief thought
can cover it

It is deep however

So deep
scientists
cannot measure
its depth

When a rock star
approaches the mic

Looks left

Looks right

Then

    One!

        Two!

           Three!

              Four!

That slight distance
between *Four!*
and music
holds whole universes

I love rock n roll
put another dime
in the jukebox baby

I Wonder Where I Wander?

My mind often wanders to places I have been
but can no longer find
These memories come to me
unbidden and without a clear map

A stretch of road on a highway
that curves above and away from a river
Crossing from one state to another

But where?
A clear image can't seem to form

I find it the same,
when the flash of a trendy bar in a big city,
the place to be, I recall, flutters in then out again

What bar?

Which big city?

Snatches of memory come and go of their own volition
There it is, the supper club we somehow found
well off the interstate
driving to find a new home in a new city

Somewhere

Somewhere is where I have been but where I cannot say
It seems I am but a mind wanderer
with no clear destination

I am here but where?

I am there but when?

A poet without GPS or *Google Maps*

Items I MUST Take When I Travel

1 Camera(s)

Always my cell phone camera, which is great for snapshots and reference photos I might paint/draw later. If it is a memorable trip to a destination, then I will include my Sony Cyber-Shot.

2 Sketchbook

Over the past 24 years, my sketchbooks have become an extension of myself. They serve as both art form and journals.

3 Drawing/painting materials...

This includes graphite pencils, black ink pens (I prefer the Uni-ball gel pens, they dry quickly and don't smear), small pan watercolor set(s), several brushes, small plastic jar w/cap for watercolors, blending sticks, sharpener, kneaded erasures, and a straight edge. If I'm on an extended trip, I often carry a canvas pad and a set of acrylic paints.

4 Handy little items...

like tissues, lip gloss, cough drops, etc.

5 How does it all fit?

Each art item fits in flat zipper cases, which in turn fit into another flat case. All of this travels conveniently in my rolling backpack.

I'm ready to travel!

Things I Told My Boys (A Roadmap)

Each person born into this world is presented a roadmap to the life they might live. A map with lines drawn by fathers, mothers, countless ancestors crossing generations and continents.

Lines drawn over lines, but not set in stone. It is your portion to either trod the known path or draw fresh lines on the map you receive.

When you (each) were born, I told you, "I love you."
I did, I do.

Late at night, I sang to you over and over hoping you would remember.
You don't.

When you reached for a hot knob or fell into the thorns,
I wanted to protect you.
Yet, you chart your own course, you draw new lines on your map.

When you were off to school, I walked you to the bus the first day. After, you walked yourselves. Each day I sent you off with the phrase, "you are handsome, and you are smart."

You are.

Traditional pot
stirring spoon
sculpture, 2017

I instilled in you the best road map I know.

But the map you chart is your map. Fresh lines drawn over old marks. A journey only you will forge. On trails, you choose to travel.

My father presented me a roadmap.

He drew a map that respected kindness to others, and toughness in one's self. Mostly it was a wonderful map. However, he walked paths I have chosen not to. Those roads were, for me, a dead end.

I credit my father with showing me the way. And, just as important for showing me the way not to travel.

Choose not to follow. Choose NOT to stay on a preordained path. Choices to follow, or not to follow, are essential to the future, you. The single self that can chart a new road, new byway, and highway is you.

In the scheme of each person's roadmap, decisions along the pathways of life often place us at a crossroads. Forward? Left? Right? It is our lot to draw new lines or follow old ones.

You choose the lines you draw on the roadmap of YOUR journey.

On the Road to Sonoma

Uber arrives
load lots of luggage

Driver is a no go
luggage lifted out

Chagrined passengers
left standing curbside

New Uber
load lots of luggage

Our journey begins

Pause for road work

Steam roller passes like some giant beast
escaped from its cage

Weathered tree collapsed on a hillside
branches look like dinosaur bones

We slither along a snake trail of concrete two-lane then four,
two then four, then two

Rounded hills pulsing the greenest green from recent rains are
periodically punctuated by carpets of colorful wildflowers.

Rows of grapevines ascend hills and follow valleys into wine country.

Read

   Watch

      Sleep

        Wake

          Smile

           Sonoma

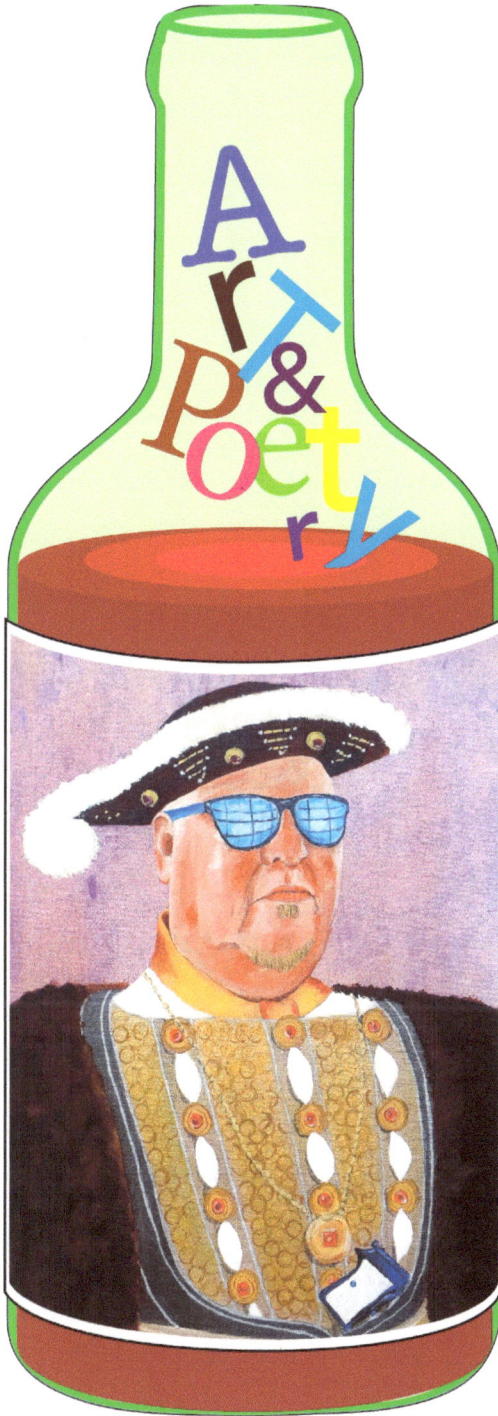

Portrait
of the
Artist as
Henry
the VIII,
2015

50¢ Worth

Rummaging for a purpose long forgotten
your hand emerges clasping a shining silver disk

Is that a Ben Franklin?
my curiosity always peaked by the unusual

In the complete insouciance of innocence
and carelessness of youth you proffer the collectible

Intent on our evening parting I slip the treasure into my blues
where it's memory will be lost, by you, to time

Both memory and coin are with me yet
a trivial gesture enduring decades and world wanderings

How this small item (and that moment) endured
remains a mystery that mirrors our journey of two

Like an endowment your casual investment multiplied
the value of a Franklin maturing twenty-fold

A pittance that a Grand Canyon of treasure
could not measure the yield on your 50¢ worth

Dancing with the Trees

Come out! Come out!
said she
and listen to the wind

We stood in the dark on the deck
watching bare winter trees
sway in the warming wind

We danced with the trees
made bold by the freedom
of darkness

Remember said she
when we would dance naked
on nights like this

Yes
it's a bit cold
I demurred

She, smiling,
even so you would have
done it then

Yes
I would have

I did
then

Walkin'
on
Sunshine, 2011

In the 11th Hour

I am in deep purple
sailing through Kentucky fog
Hush, hush
Rush

In the 11th hour of my sojourn
seeking my queen
Gee, I think you're swell
my pride and joy, etc.

So many ask
why don't you rest?
Motel, hotel?
oh, hell no
gotta go, go

I drive on alone
but never lonely
With me are Mamas, Papas,
Monkees, Zombies & Turtles

Behind me, rolls our past
which I am driving
into our future

The oldies keep on rockin'
I keep on rollin'
into the 12th hour
closer to the one I love

I'm running on empty
Build me up Buttercup
don't break my heart

Young Lovers on a Plane

I see them as they stumble down the aisle
staying close bumping each other so not to lose contact
parting only to slip into their seats

Gazing with new discovery they kiss
then kiss again and yet once more
holding this kiss to linger on their lips

As the silver chariot wings away
she sleeps head snuggled on his shoulder
stirs awakens. They kiss once more

The plane pauses in mid-flight
resuming only when their lips part
young love floats young love flies

Wear your love like heaven

Jasmine
at
NARA,
2015

You Take My Breath Away

You were thirteen and I a bit older when we danced and
You take my breath away

You were merely nineteen when you spoke "I do" and
You take my breath away

Time went by as time will do, you bore my babies and
You take my breath away

By sun's rays and candlelight
You take my breath away

From the Heartland to the Atlantic across to the Pacific,
from Mexico to Canada
You take my breath away

I sighed in Italy, smiled in Ireland, was awe struck in Africa and
You take my breath away

Time went by as time will and in the morning preparing for your
bath you paused in the doorway framed by the morning sun.

I stopped to gaze and
You take my breath away

What remittance will you bestow
for the countless breaths
I've held when I see you?

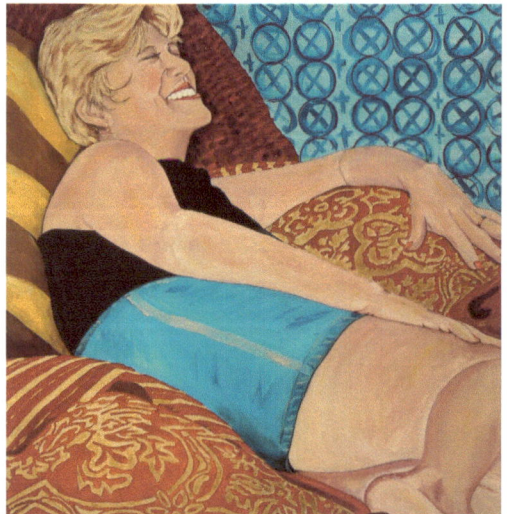

Odalisque
in
Blue Shorts,
2008

A Letter to My Wife

Sometimes, on a bright crisp morning,
I think of our first house in Des Moines.

Saturdays we'd listen to football games
on the radio while we worked together.

I might be driving down the street and
smile, thinking of breakfast in that cafe
in Killarney, billowing curtains in Rome,
dinners in New Orleans, and Victoria Falls
where we chased two monkeys from our room.

Occasionally, when it's cold, a thought
flits through my head I see you sleeping
on the floor, Christmas in Kansas, cold, so cold,
pregnant and beautiful, so beautiful.

Rummaging through a drawer I come upon
a photo of one of the boys when they were
small. So many experiences, so many memories...

These things can't be bought with money
and can't be measured by height and width.

They can only be purchased and measured
through the long perspective of time.

Love is an inadequate and small word.
Partnership and devotion are better.

Laughing, crying, holding your head when
you are sick. When tragedy hits, seeing pain
in your eyes and bringing your pain into my
heart. All of these things, and so much more,
you have given to me and I to you.

Some ask, *is it hard?*
No, I say, *it's easy.*

Just get up every day
and go forward, together.

I Felt Your Touch

I was sleeping when I felt you touch my hair
the sensation seemed to come from nowhere

Softly you brushed my temple as you sometimes do
Strange, because I am flying to see you

You are much on my mind
I nodded off on the plane,
but you were neither in front of me nor behind

You came to me not in a dream,
but in the manifestation of a reality
as real as any schizophrenic's voice, a totality

Even though we are not together I felt your touch,
What is this curious voodoo?
No matter where I go you are with me, it must be your hoodoo

You reach through time and space
to do that thing
you do do, to me

Here's Lookin'
at
You, 2012

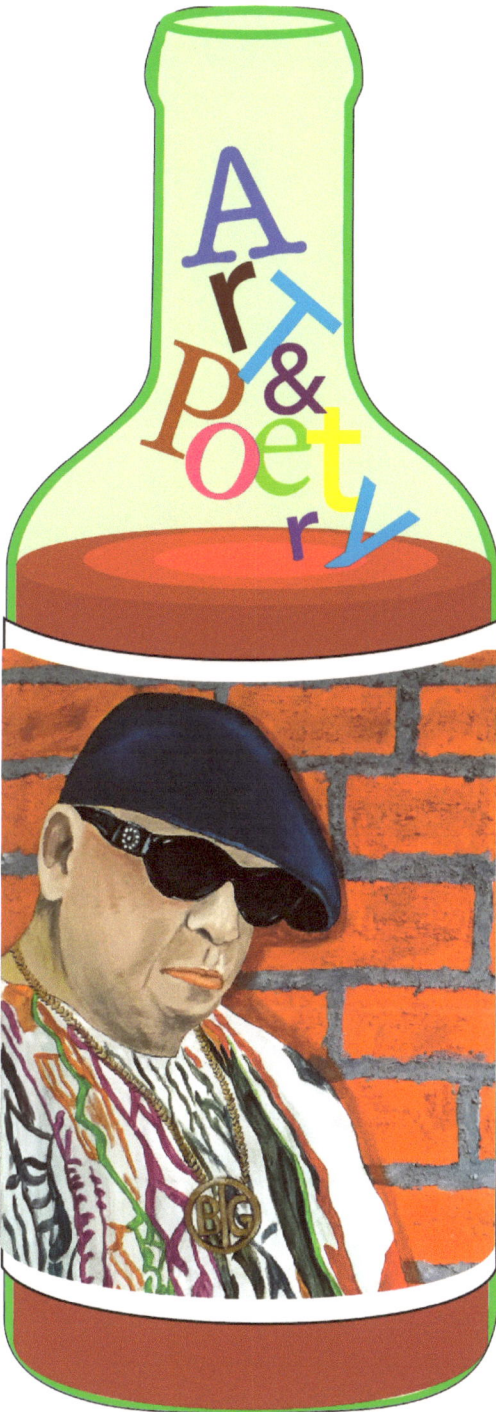

Portrait of
the Artist
as Biggie
Smalls,
2016

Art & Poetry

PEOPLE

The Madonna of the Train

She sleeps without care
of one without sin
this Madonna of the Train

Surrounded by hundreds
traveling to the city of millions

The multitude boards silently
eyes downcast empty hands
clutching clutter and caffeine

Settling into spaces like so many ghosts
the inevitable query is lofted

Does this train go to New York?

Inevitable answer is batted back

It better be, I am.

Quiet laughter, then
Yes, this is the train to New York.

GOD SPEAKS:

**"Next stop Orange.
Only stop before New York Penn Station"**

Read, sleep, rock with the rhythm,
the Madonna sleeps on

GOD INTONES:

**"Next stop New York Penn Station
take your clutter, mind the gap."**

The Madonna awakens
the multitude becomes energized

We stride into Penn Station and are beatified
in the light of a new, New York morning

Madonna
of the Train
Stippled pen
drawing, 2009

Truck Stop Seasoning

In truck stops across America
food is seasoned with
salt-of-the-earth women

Who serve you and
pepper conversations
with the same phrases:

Coffee hon?

Where 'ya all from?

Where 'ya headed?

That's a fer piece.

Ready to order?

Can I get you anything else?

Thanks Hon,
    You travel safe now.

The script has been long written
and each delivers their lines
without pause or flaw.

Across America

The same men sit at
every truck stop in America.

They chew slowly and smoke
with a purpose.

Alone, they sit pensively,
as if still on the road.

Together, they lean into each
other in animated conversation.

There are only two waitresses
in all of the country:

Honey and Doll.

They work very hard.

You Were Always Happy in the Morning

The hair of your ancestors proclaimed your fierce temper
but you were always happy in the morning
I am told when you and dad wed you were inseparable lovers
You the buxom farm girl and dad the world-class athlete
that must have been something to see
but time, children, and life-long poverty
dulled the shine on that apple

Even so, you were always happy in the morning
By the time I was twelve the war at home was full-blown
pots and skillets thrown but your words hit harder than metal
Mornings you were always the first to arise
in the kitchen with the coffee on and radio
playing so softly I needed to stand close to hear
the weather and futures

You were always happy in the morning
Dad already outside in the dark at work
I too off into the cold or heat to chore
then back inside the kitchen with you
where hot coffee, oatmeal, and quiet chats awaited

You were always happy in the morning
I learned to love those early beginnings spent with you
For the next six years the battles erupted
Gentle mornings followed by lonely days
and the nightly mêlées that could turn from
words to blows and then resignation

Yet, you were happy in the mornings
At least I think you were
I was gone into the world forging my own path
a journey without oatmeal and you

I would visit in the mornings
because that's when you were happiest
we'd sip burnt coffee perking for five hours

I'd talk about my job and wife
I'd bring you my latest art to show
you'd listen and nod or frown speaking quietly without judgement

When the cancer came you were not happy (even in the mornings)
You seethed against Dad and God
the injustice deemed too much
Then when your voice failed you snarled your condemnation
the priest quailed before your wrath

You died on a sunny spring morning slipping away as quietly as
one of our longed-for talks
No more quiet conversations
No more burnt coffee
I miss that and you, of course
but its good you passed at daybreak
You were always happy in the morning.

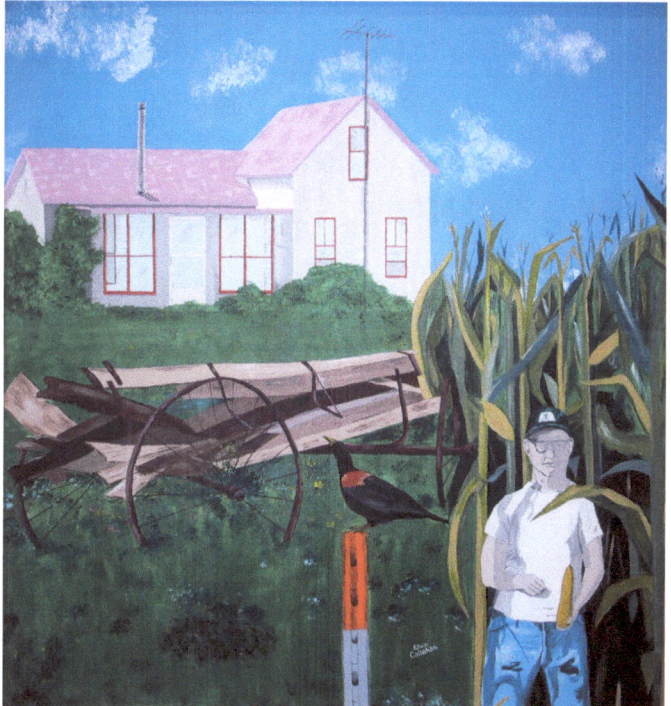

Portrait
of my Mother,
1994

The Collector

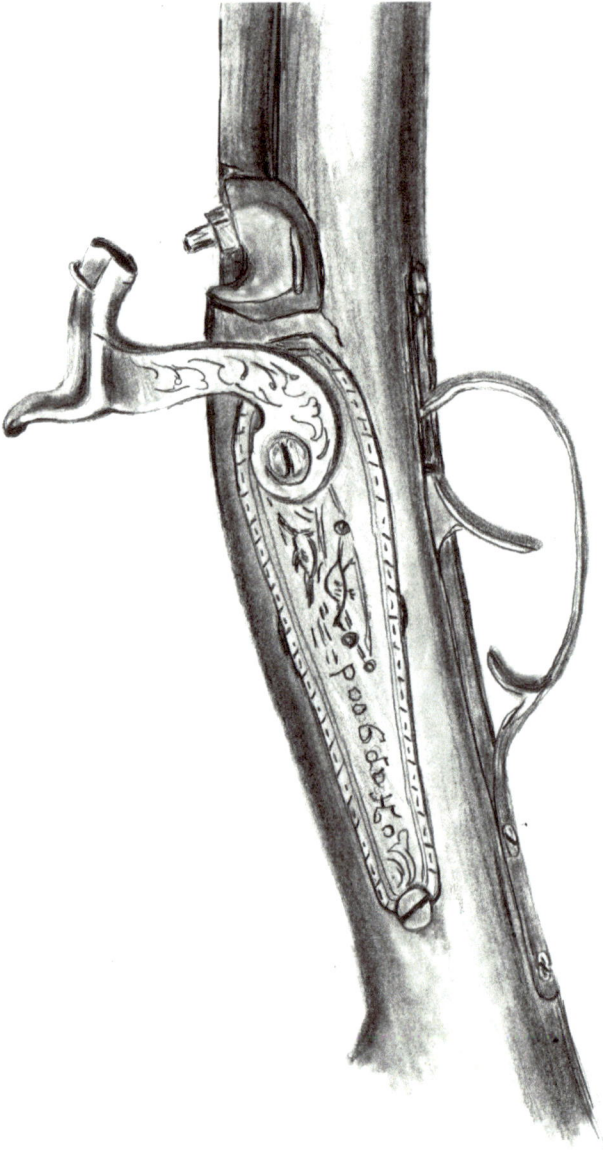

An aficionado
I collect them,
these modern-day
Ivanhoes
Natty Bumpos
and Chuck Heston
look-a-likes

They are all [each]
tall, broad of shoulder
and
sharp of eye
you would want them
to be your friend

But,
they are
not
yours
they are
mine

They each
gather to
me
as moths to a flame

They come
to be with
their
diminutive
General of the Plains

Hapgood Musket
Graphite drawing,
1998

Arriving
on wings of burnished metal
and chariots that speed cross the land
they gather like ancient Greek warriors
on the Plains of Troy

They carry only the finest of arms,
drink strong spirits
and
eat rich foods served
in the temple by the gods
Apollo and Daphne

They [each]
have goddesses of their own
with children and
their children's children

They [each]
gather from across
the breadth and width
of this great land

They come to
me,
where
I walk among
them
as a man might through
a tall forest of mighty men

My friends
My companions of the field
My life-long collection
gods of my heart

Mother Could Shoot

My mother Ruby, was a fiery redhead. She was generous of heart but also had a quick temper. One thing few knew about Mom was that she could shoot. In the front yard of our first farm, there was a row of pine trees that grew close together and had low hanging branches that brushed the ground. Often, especially on cold winter mornings, we would discover the lower branches lined with pheasants huddled out of the wind. If Mom were in the mood for a fresh bird, she would merely stick the shotgun out of the door and fire away. Us boys were then directed to clean the birds for dinner.

I was born on that farm and lived there until I was twelve years old. The most memorable feature was the lack of indoor plumbing. One tends to remember this, especially in the winter,

when I am most thankful for the five bathrooms I have in my current home. I remember every speck of black dirt and every dusty cobweb in the corners of the buildings. I remember the shrieking of the old windmill that pumped the water up for the cattle. And the house-lot sized garden we kept in the summer. Oh, there is so much I remember.

For several years we had a Hereford bull we named Sammy. Sammy was as gentle as he was massive. When Sammy would lay down in the pasture in his majestic repose, my brother and I would clamber all over him, petting his ears and perching on his tabletop sized back. He would never move a muscle until we were off his back and safely away. Sammy became a character in another of my stories.

Years ago, 1999 if I remember correctly, I drove out to the old place and was pleased to see the old barn was still standing. The first barn burnt in 1948, under mysterious circumstances, before I was born. My father and grandfather rebuilt the one that still stands as I write this. I spent the afternoon recording it in my sketchbook.

I remember milking cows in that old barn and sometimes squirting the milk into the mewing cat's mouths. I remember Old Joe Probasco lining a steer up against the side of the barn where Joe would shoot it from about five feet away with a single shot from a .22 rifle. In my youthful exuberance, I would always shout, "Good shot, Joe!" The steer then butchered into steaks, hamburger, and roasts in the nearby shed. We had no money, but we ate well.

Iowa Barn
Graphite
drawing,
1999

Traffic Jam in Aisle 13

Large ladies labor
with maddening slowness
in the lanes of the local 'Mart

Blocking all passage
pausing every few steps to
gaze into the maw of merchandise
as if each item held the answer
to the mysteries of the universe

When (I suspect)
they are really thinking:
     "pink?
     or purple?"

WWJP?
(What would Jesus pick?)

Waiting,
2009

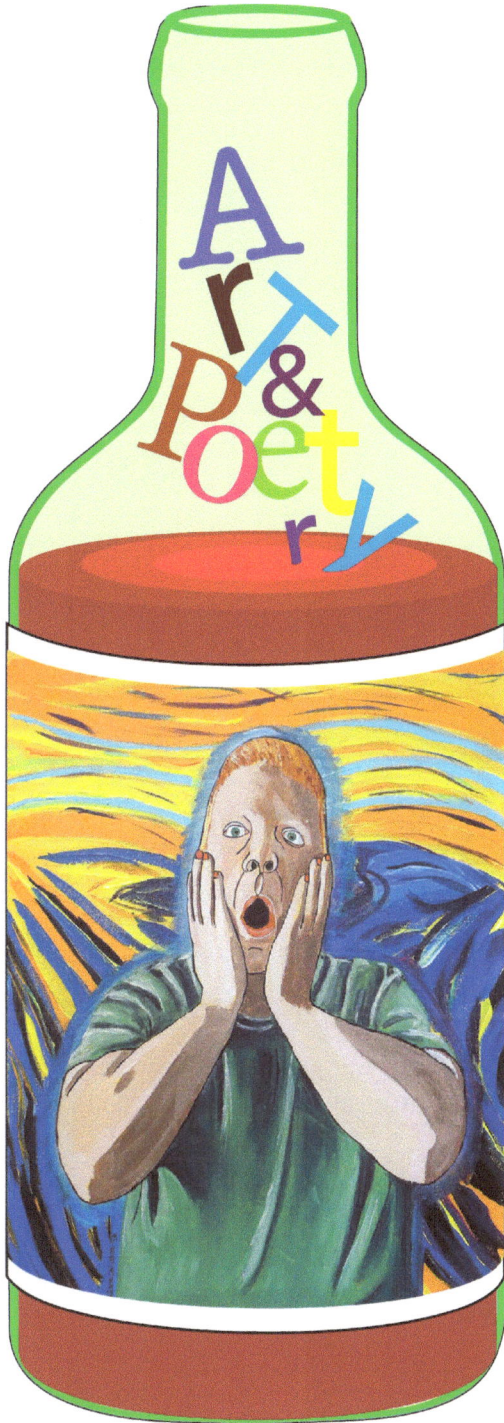

Portrait of the Artist as Munch's The Scream, 2016

The Bright Spark of a High Heeled Boy

Michael and Ross, or just *the Boys* entered our
lives through a small act of kindness
One apartment condemned the other not built
Both became our guests for a time

Ross is an artist, tall, spare, quiet
At rest, his body folds like a living origami
cigarette held casually between his fingers
glows like the scepter of a young prince

Struck by this physicality
his image ensnared in an unguarded moment
but how to capture the enigmatic soul of the artist
on canvas?

Slashing and dripping, color covers
the life-sized canvas,
I reach back half a century to the POP style
his likeness rendered in the abstract flat colors
indicated contours

Somehow the brush finds Ross
serendipitously the face intertwines
with the background
exquisitely illuminating the subject's
inscrutable qualities

In this portrait of a high heeled boy
there is the bright human spark of
a man, an artist, and a friend

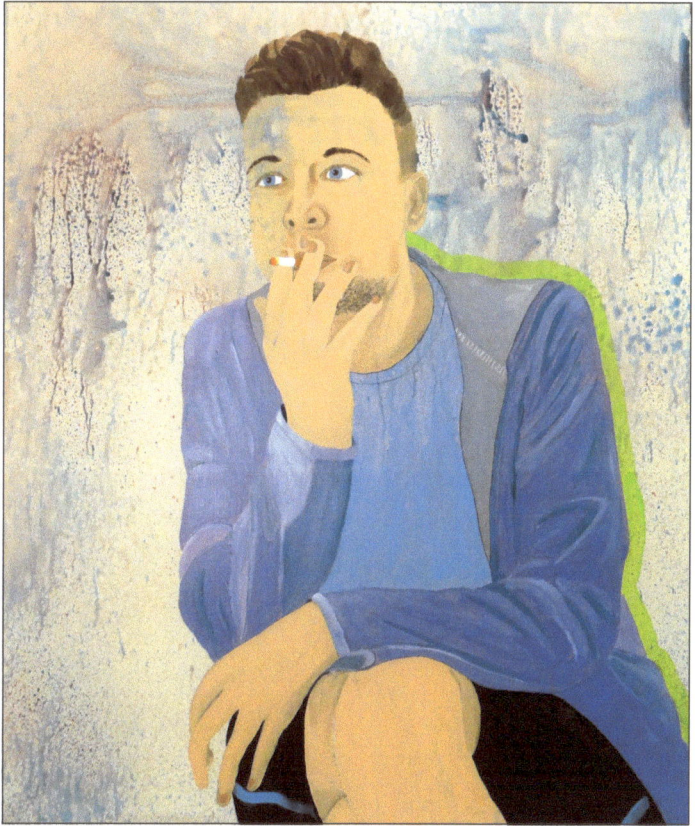

Portrait of the
Artist
Ross Redmon,
2016

Perfect Work of Art

Through the window of my painting studio
winter sky is framed like a fine work of art

Sycamore branches look like old bare bones
trembling in an arctic breeze
dancing on one foot, shivering in nakedness

The trees are solitary not leaf nor bird for companion
alone in a cloudless sky of over-mixed watercolor

I am at once struck by this stark beauty
Then the realization that I will never create
such a perfect work of art with my hands

White Room

Tried, judged, convicted and sentenced for my crimes.
Or perhaps it was for my sins?
I am never sure.

I never saw those who judged me, nor heard the testimony given.

Sentenced to a white room from which there would be no reprieve
– my punishment, a cell: blindingly white.

My confinement diabolical, I was given no objects, no furniture,
nothing of color except the pigment of my hands.

Art is my life, writing, drawing, painting, observing. Now, only
white smooth walls, a penance devised to take everything from
me, to drive me insane.

Every hour, minute, moment I am falling into an abyss,
floating in a formless nowhere.

Lingering on the edge of madness for untold hours, days, months,
perhaps even years
(I can no longer tell) I lay with eyes closed, conjuring color, line,
shapes, movement.

It began slowly, tentatively, pulling on my fingertip until I began
to bleed *Color.* The vermillion paint at first only oozes but soon it
becomes a steady stream fed by the pounding of my heart.

Pollock-drops of red paint the floor when I cross the room and
begin to paint on my only canvas.

The image begins with my feet, legs lifting up to float and
undulate like Chagall's smitten husband. The background Klimt-
like wallpaper.

Around I sketch, drawing legs, hands, arms, body. I slap, smear,
and push volume, shape, form.

A screaming depiction of my face emerges from my mind and
appears on the surface. Completing the circle of the cell, at last,
I connect head to foot.

My "Guernica" is nearing completion. Weak, sans the liquid of life I need only a few more drops to sign my name just as light is extinguished.

White and drained of color my body is desiccated. I leave behind the only true thing I have to give this world, the color they attempted to squelch.

A professed martyr to the cause, born to art, condemned to create.

Gradually awareness returns, surrounded by half-empty tubes of paint, still dripping brushes.
I survey the results of my latest work and see that I once again have won the war of the canvas.

Portrait of the Artist as Michelangelo, 2016

Perfect Squares

Kazimir

Georges

Piet Diego

Juan Pablo

Squares all

Perfect cubes for an ism

As scene at the MoMA

Peggy
Guggenheim's
Bed,
2013

On Making Art

At age four
I began making art

I made art
for myself

*Well, your
mother will like it*

Meaning my work
is accepted by
family and friends

Important words
to buoy any artist

But to fly
to
Grow

One must leave
the golden glow
of the familiar

Seek
wider praise

*The glow
for me has
dimmed*

But still
I make art

Alone
I make art
in obscurity

Opining to
another artist
I quipped

There is support for
*Jewish artists
Black artists
Hispanic artists
Women artists
Gay artists
Emerging artists*

*But
Who supports
Old-Fat-Pale artists?*

We laugh
and resume
our making

I make art
for my mother (again)
She would love my art
(were she yet alive)

So...

I

make

art

for

Myself

Compliments

My paintbrush
picks up paint

and brushes
the canvas

The canvas
returns the
compliment

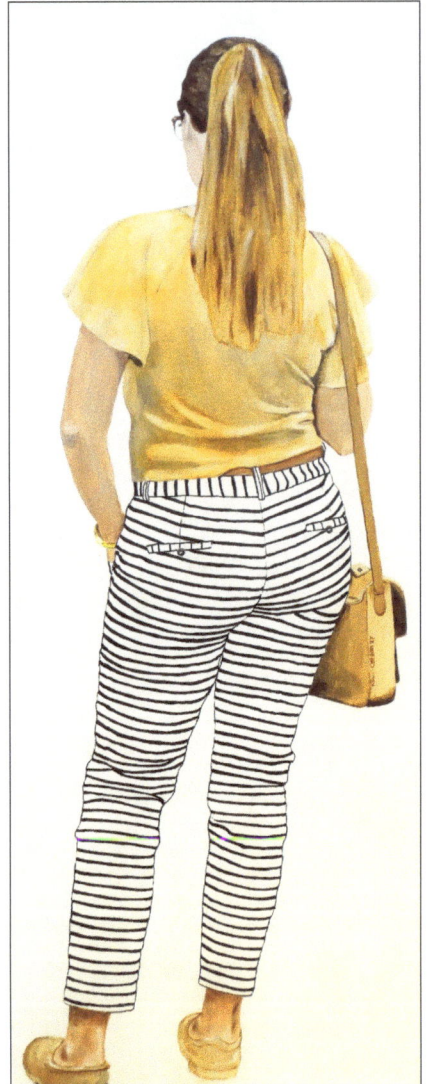

Barcelona MoMA,
Stripped Girls
Series, 2017

Paul Klee
Flying
Continental, 2014

How to Make a Walking Stick

I have been told that a walking stick is a metaphor for my life? Well, perhaps. A walking stick can be many things, so I suppose a metaphor is not out of the question.

1) The first step is to find a suitable stick. Finding the right stick (for you) will necessarily require that you get out of the house and walk (unaided) in Mother Nature. Figure out how long you want your stick then cut to length.

A walking stick is a reminder that there is another world outside, off the beaten path. Your silent stick is also a gentle prompt to use it and discover those many places where you can travel.

2) Trim and then "skin" your stick with a sharp knife. CAREFUL, don't trim your own digits.

Your personal walking aid will steady you on a rough path, serve as a probe to make sure you don't tread on anything nasty, and give a rest on which to lean while you admire the view from the top.

3) Smooth the wood and remove bumps and scratches.

A tranquil walk will serve to remove the everyday bumps and scratches of life, smoothing out your mind and body.

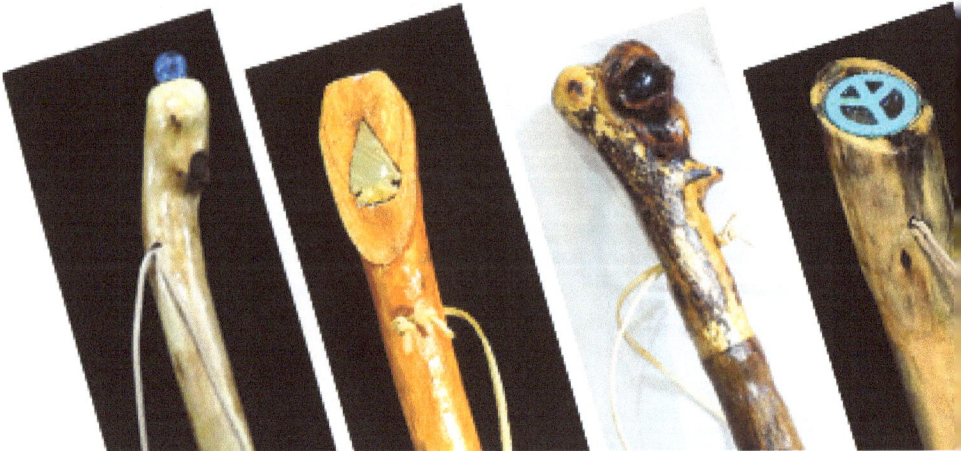

4) Finish your stick with a protective coat.

A nature walk with your stick is akin to adding a finishing coat on both body and soul.

5) It's time to "top off" your creation. That is very much up to your imagination. I often look for old Sycamore knots as they weather into fantastic shapes and attach easily.

In so many ways, my walking sticks are everything I have described and more. But as for metaphor, I believe my poetry, stories, and art have been my walking sticks, guiding me along the paths of my life.

6) Enjoy your custom walking stick for many years to come.

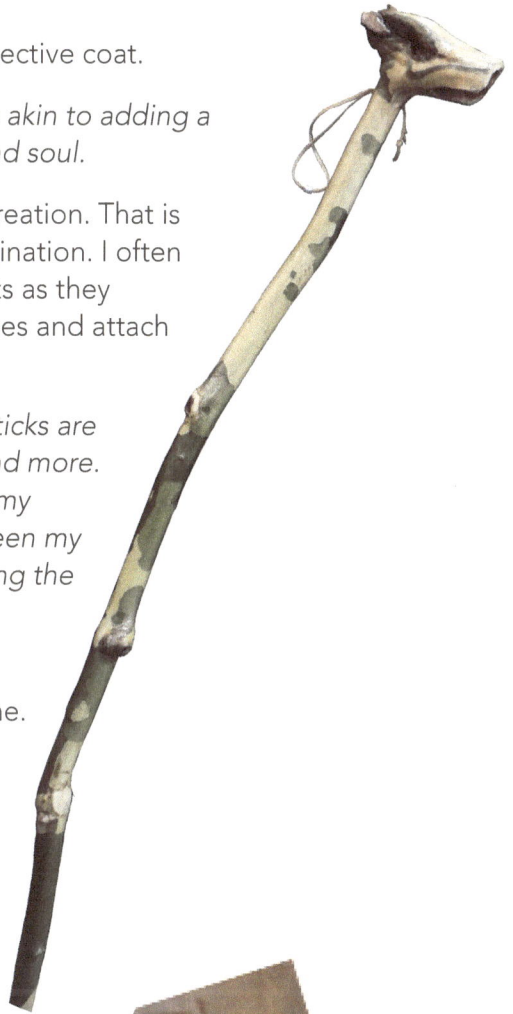

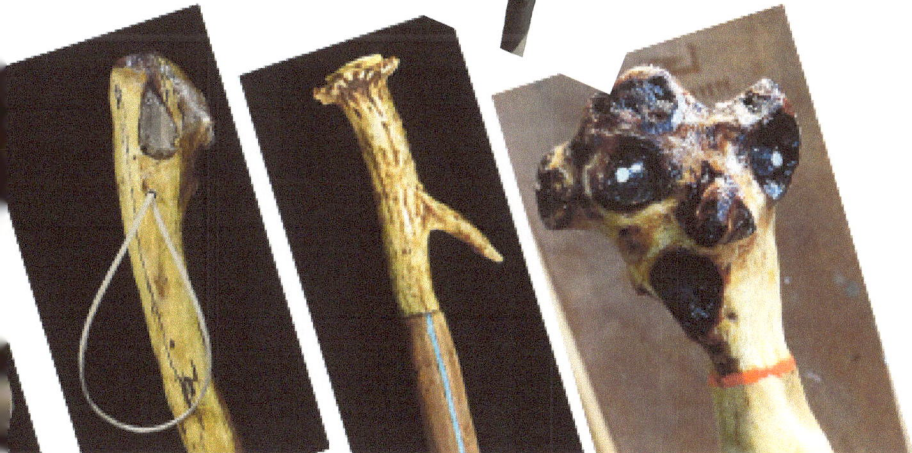

This poem is placed at the end to celebrate the author's beginnings. Every journey must have its roots. Thank you for reading and looking.

Once Was

The old house sits in the countryside. Ancient and abandoned, its only nod to past elegance, an incongruous red door: the bright beacon encircled by peeling-paint walls, broken windows, and head-high weeds.

But this house once was a country castle for a farmer and his family. One only needs to close their eyes and imagine. Imagine what once was.

Once was a warm summer day, the drive filled with cars, tables groaning under the weight of food sitting under the shading elms whose limbs whisper softly, the summer breeze playing its music through the branches.

Children race through the yard, around and around the buildings, shouting with joy at their new-found freedom, women sit chatting about children/recipes/husbands while the men occupy another space/place and the talk is crops/animals/tractors/prices.

Once was when Fall arrived cool, fat, and promising; the pasture filled with going-to-market cattle. Ham and bacon on the hoof snorted and wallowed in pens adjacent to a barn filled with summer-cut hay. The surrounding country fairly aquiver with the anticipation of the harvest soon to come.

Once was/always is, the passing of time. Graduations/far-off schools/weddings/babies, then (as time will pass) children gone to discover their lives elsewhere. Those were the quiet years for the house. The shouts and laughter only an echo bouncing around silent rooms.

Once was when the house welcomed home its progeny. But the day came when the return was only to pay last respects. And so, the home that once was sits. Inevitably, it too will make way for another acre of crops. Only the ghost of the house will remain.

Once was the day I happened upon the relic, lured by the red door against winter white. I captured it with camera, so it will live on forever in my photograph and these few words, a silent monument to a rural past. A different time in America.

Once was.

Once Was
Digital photo,
2014

About the Author

Kēvin (pronounced Keevin) Callahan calls himself the "Accidental Poet" as most of his poetry appears to him at odd times. His work is colored by his upbringing on a rural Iowa farm, his family, and extensive travel around the US, Canada, Mexico, Europe, and Africa.

Kēvin Callahan is an award-winning writer, painter, photographer, poet, and sculptor. His writings include one self-published novel, *Morris' Code*, two anthologies of non-fiction short stories, *A Prairie Wind Blowing Through My Head*, a collection of stories about his youth on an Iowa farm, and *A Day Remembered*, stories of his years in the field pursuing upland game. His fictional *Chinese Checkers Run*, is an exciting adventure story of flight and pursuit. All available on Kindle.

At a Painting Intensive at the San Francisco Art Institute he studied painting with world renown Israeli artist Larry Abramson and at the Ox-Bow School of the Art Institute Chicago under Phil Hanson and Michelle Grabner.

Photo credit: Julia Reynolds

His poems and art have been published in numerous anthologies. His numerous short stories often appear in his hometown newspaper.

Callahan earned a BFA from Drake University in Des Moines, IA. His work hangs in private collections throughout the world.

Kēvin currently works and resides with his wife in Parkville, MO and both of his sons are accomplished artists.

For more info contact the author at kevin@bsfgadv.com

Kēvin Callahan- *"I am a maker of the artifacts of ancient man."*

I have been constructing reproductions of primitive artifacts since I was a young boy on an Iowa farm. I have since turned my passion for the primitive into works of art.

Sculptures that "Might" be Spoons

When is a spoon, not a spoon? When it's a sculpture. Kēvin uses wood found primarily on his property to create one-of-a-kind keepsakes. The "spoons" recall an earlier time, perhaps when pioneers pushed out onto the prairies, or in a time of magic when wizards conjured spells. Many of these creations carry overtones of The Hobbit or shades of Harry Potter. These objet d'art are meant for decoration only, as the oils used to enhance and restore the wood are not for human consumption.

Objet D'art (Home Decor)

Unique wood items to decorate your home. Handmade from forest woods, old barns, and shells, these items will find a treasured place in any home.

Walking Sticks

When out for a walk in the park or a hike through Mother Nature's beauty, a good stick is essential. Pretty much any old stick will do, so you say. I say, why not be fashion-forward and use a stick that makes a statement? One that fits your needs, style, and budget. I road test each of my walking sticks before they are posted for sale

Prairie Primitives
Handmade Artistry from the Heartland

prairieprimitive.net

www.ingramcontent.com/pod-product-compliance
Lightning Source LLC
LaVergne TN
LVHW010023070426
835508LV00001B/15